Project Manager:
Charles Payne, M.A., M.F.A.

Editor in Chief:
Sharon Coan, M.S. Ed.

Art Director:
Elayne Roberts

Art Coordination Assistant:
Cheri Macoubrie Wilson

Cover Artist:
Larry Bauer

Product Manager:
Phil Garcia

Imaging:
Ralph Olmedo Jr.

Publishers:
Rachelle Cracchiolo, M.S. Ed.
Mary Dupuy Smith, M.S. Ed.

Simple Internet Activities

Author:

Alain Chirinian

Teacher Created Materials, Inc.
6421 Industry Way
Westminster, CA 92683
ISBN-1-57690-460-1
©1999 Teacher Created Materials, Inc.
Reprinted, 2000
Made in U.S.A.
www.teachercreated.com
URL updates available at our Web site.

Table of Contents

Introduction

This book is designed to take full advantage of an important new learning opportunity now available to our students: the Internet. While many teachers are becoming plugged into the Internet, they are often at a loss at to how students can use it on a consistent basis and in a self-guided manner. *Simple Internet Activities* provides a teacher with real online activities that go beyond a simple "scavenger hunt." These carefully selected Web sites contain innovative, exciting activities that can be completed online in a variety of subject areas. Science, math, language arts, social studies, and art are well represented with a variety of entertaining and informative Web sites that open the door for further exploration using puzzles, games, and links to related sites—and that's just the beginning!

Modern educational theory and experience have taught us that students learn best when they see and interact with a subject using as many modalities as possible. These carefully selected activities allow you and the students to do just that by supplementing your curriculum and increasing student enthusiasm, retention, and performance in each topic.

Each page is a self-contained endeavor that can be completed in less than a standard class period. Students complete the online and written portions simultaneously, using many of their skills and developing new ones as they progress through the book. Teacher pages prior to each activity will give you suggestions regarding the appropriate use of the activity and potential extensions in class.

Simple Internet Activities assumes that you have a basic knowledge of Internet use and terminology and can move freely around the Web as needed. It is important that you upgrade your browser to the latest version available and enable its *Java* capabilities. Furthermore, you should take advantage of the many available helper applications, or "plug-ins," such as *Shockwave* and *RealAudio* for best results on some Web sites.

Finally, always double-check that the Web site or links from a Web site are still active before you assign an activity. With the fast pace of change on the Internet, some sites may have moved or disappeared altogether in the interim since this book was written.

Wave Your Flag High!

Teacher Notes

Additional Content Area(s):

- social studies
- math

Objectives:

Students will

- determine the flag code for maritime flags.
- create a message using maritime flag codes.

Materials Required:

- computer with Internet access
- pencil or pen
- colored pencils, pens, or markers
- ruler

Web Site(s):

http://www.wln.com/~deltapac/flags.html

http://www3.fast.co.za/~alistair/flags~1.htm

Time Required:

- 25–30 minutes

Teaching the Lesson:

- Begin the lesson with a discussion of the need for maritime flags in an era with unreliable or nonexistent radio communications. See if students can determine what some important maritime messages might have been.
- Be sure that students double-check the meanings of the flags they draw. They should be aware that grammatical structure is only approximate when creating messages with maritime flags.

Name: _____ Date: _____

Wave Your Flag High!

Flag-waving has been one way sailors communicate with each other from ship to ship long before there was radio.

Go to:

http://www.wln.com/~deltapac/flags.html

Look at the message from the flags on this Web page.

Go to:

http://www3.fast.co.za/~alistair/flags~1.htm

Find out how to draw and color flags that say the following message:

"Do not pass me; I have a man overboard!"

On the back of this sheet, draw and color the flags. Then, make up a short message and see if your neighbor can read it!

Ad-lib Your Madlibs!

Teacher Notes

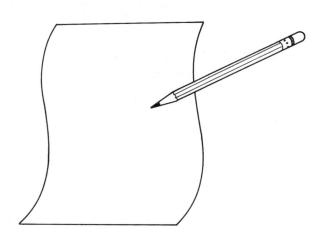

Objectives:

Students will

- identify parts of speech.
- create a story using different parts of speech.

Materials Required:

- computer with Internet access
- pencil or pen

Web Site(s):

http://www.ugcs.caltech.edu/cgi/~wart/pick_madlib.pl

Time Required:

- 25 minutes

Teaching the Lesson:

- Students may need a refresher on parts of speech for this activity.
- Be sure to give students individual help as they create their own stories and delete various parts of speech. They can then simply switch papers with their neighbors to create new stories.

Name: _____ Date: _____

Ad-lib Your Madlibs!

At this Web site, you will be asked for words that function as different parts of speech such as nouns, verbs, adverbs, and adjectives. The words you enter will be placed in a story online at this Web page. See how your story turns out!

Go to:

http://www.ugcs.caltech.edu/cgi/~wart/pick_madlib.pl

Write below the list of words you placed in each blank space on the Web page.

Part of Speech	Word
_____	_____
_____	_____
_____	_____
_____	_____
_____	_____
_____	_____
_____	_____
_____	_____
_____	_____

Now make up your own fill-in-the-blank story! Write a story that is one or two paragraphs long. Then remove some of the nouns, verbs, adverbs, and adjectives. Be sure to label each blank space as the same part of speech you just erased. Have your neighbor fill in the blank spaces and then read the stories out loud for fun!

Your Words, Your Story

Teacher Notes

Objectives:

Students will

- identify parts of speech.
- create a story with amusing content.

Materials Required:

- computer with Internet access
- pencil or pen

Web Site(s):

http://www.eduplace.com/tales/burp.html

Time Required:

- 25 minutes

Teaching the Lesson:

- This Web site provides, in some detail, an opportunity for a primer on parts of speech. If time permits, all students should review this material.
- Creating the final product (a funny story) during this activity is a good way to learn about different writing styles, elements of humor, etc.
- You can explore the other stories on this Web site for similar activities if you wish to do more of them.

Name: _____ Date: _____

Your Words, Your Story

Your teacher may want you to click on the "review parts of speech" button. Otherwise, be sure you know what nouns, verbs, adjectives, and other parts of speech are before you begin this activity.

Go to:

---

http://www.eduplace.com/tales/burp.html

Fill in the words in each blank space on this Web page. Click "see your Wacky Web Tale" when you are finished. Read the story you have just created. Was it funny? See if you can make it a funny story by writing the same story below with a different set of words.

_____

_____

_____

_____

_____

_____

_____

_____

_____

_____

_____

_____

Define and Conquer!

Teacher Notes

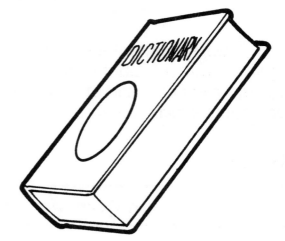

Objectives:

Students will

- use context clues to define words.
- create sentences using newly defined words.

Materials Required:

- computer with Internet access
- pencil or pen

Web Site(s):

http://www.eduplace.com/dictionary/index.html

Time Required:

- 25–30 minutes

Teaching the Lesson:

- A discussion/lesson on defining words using context clues is a good way to simplify the instructions in this activity.
- Be sure that students record the words and correct definition of each word on the student page.
- Naturally, student sentences should be original, not a rewording of the definition. You can even expand on this and have them each write a story using these words to provide context clues in the story.

Name: _____ Date: _____

Define and Conquer!

Have you ever been able to guess the meaning of a word just by looking at it? Sometimes it helps to try to guess the meaning of a word when it is in a sentence. Here is your chance to make some guesses about some really wild words!

Go to:

http://www.eduplace.com/dictionary/index.html

Choose your grade level and click on a word. Click on the definition that you think is the closest match.

Make a list below of the new words that you have added to your vocabulary. Write the correct definition next to each word.

Word	**Definition**
_____	_____
_____	_____
_____	_____
_____	_____
_____	_____

Now make up a sentence containing each new word and write it below.

1. _____

2. _____

3. _____

4. _____

5. _____

One Happy Dog

Teacher Notes

Objectives:

Students will

- read a story online.
- answer comprehension questions about the story.

Materials Required:

- computer with Internet access
- pencil or pen

Web Site(s):

http://www.fogbottom.com/neighbor.html

Time Required:

- 20 minutes

Teaching the Lesson:

- This simple activity is appropriate for a slower reader or second language reader. Students can pair up and read these out loud, if appropriate, as well.
- The comprehension questions are appropriate for individuals or teamwork, again depending on the level of the reader. Structure the assignment according to individual needs for best results.

Name: _____ Date: _____

One Happy Dog

The story you will read on this Web page is about the adventures of a dog named Cool Dog Teddy. After you read the entire story, answer the questions below about what happened.

Go to:

http://www.fogbottom.com/neighbor.html

Questions

1. Does Cool Dog Teddy live in a human house or a doghouse? How do you know?

   _____

2. Why did Cool Dog Teddy growl when he first met his new neighbor?

   _____

3. What is his new neighbor's name?

   _____

4. Why was Cool Dog Teddy trying to protect his master's fish pond?

   _____

5. Even though dogs and cats are often enemies, Cool Dog Teddy got along with his new neighbor. Why do you think the two animals became friends?

   _____

6. Have you ever met a new person whom you didn't like at first and then later became friends with? Write down what happened to change your mind about that person.

   _____

Words Can't Scare You!

Teacher Notes

Objectives:

Students will

- read "scary" stories written by other students online.

- each write their own scary story in conjunction with another student.

Materials Required:

- computer with Internet access

- pencil or pen

Web Site(s):

http://www.tcfhe.com:80/goosebumps/thrillold.html

http://www.tcfhe.com:80/goosebumps/bump.html

Time Required:

- 35–50 minutes

Teaching the Lesson:

- This lesson is designed to help students learn to write using a particular genre or style—in this case "scary" stories.

- A good primer would be to brainstorm a list of "scary" words that can be used in their stories.

- The hardest part will be to have the students collaborate on their stories, one writing the beginning and one the end. They must first agree to a list of characters and use them in both parts.

- The optional activity is a reward for a good performance. It should be previewed by you to ensure it is appropriate for your students.

Name: _____ Date: _____

Words Can't Scare You!

Read the scary stories written by other students.

Can you write a scary story? Of course you can! Your assignment is to write part of a scary story. Your teacher will assign you to write either the first part or the last part of a story. Your partner will write the other part. Write your part of the scary story below. Then read them together.

Go to:

http://www.tcfhe.com:80/goosebumps/thrillold.html

_____

_____

_____

_____

_____

_____

_____

_____

_____

_____

_____

If your story was scary enough, your teacher will let you go to a fun but scary game to play. Ask your teacher for the secret **Go to** code.

It's Puzzle Time!

Teacher Notes

Objective:

Students will

- construct and solve puzzles.

Materials Required:

- computer with Internet access
- pencil or pen
- printer with paper

Web Site(s):

http://puzzlemaker.school.discovery.com/

Time Required:

- 45 minutes

Teaching the Lesson:

- This lesson is designed primarily for higher-level students to do on their own. It is appropriate to put together in teams students who may find it too challenging.
- Be sure students are comfortable printing out pages from the Internet.
- The students should use a common theme when choosing words for the word search. The secret message should be related to the theme as well.

Name: _____ Date: _____

It's Puzzle Time!

Here is your chance to baffle your friends with a puzzle designed by YOU!

The first puzzle you will make is called a cryptogram. Click on "cryptogram." A cryptogram is a secret code that changes letters into numbers or different letters.

Go to:

http://puzzlemaker.school.discovery.com/

First write a short title in the space provided. Then write the title on the line below on this paper.

_____

Then enter a short sentence that will be encrypted or written in code. Write the secret sentence on the line below on this paper.

_____

Want to give the person a head start? Choose to "give away" a few letters and type them in the space provided on the Web page. Then click "create the cryptogram." Print out the cryptogram and let your partner try to find the secret message.

Your next puzzle will be a word search with a hidden message. Use the back button on your browser to click on the button that says "word search with a hidden message." Type in the title for your puzzle. It should be about a topic you know a lot about. All the words in your word search will be about that topic. Then type in the hidden message. Finally, type the words you want in your puzzle. Type in at least 15 words about your topic. Then print out the puzzle and hand it to your neighbor! Have your neighbor write down the secret message below.

_____

Minifig Story

Teacher Notes

Additional Content Area(s):

- art

Objectives:

Students will

- create several minifigs.
- write a story about their minifigs.

Materials Required:

- computer with Internet access
- pencil or pen
- drawing/coloring supplies (optional)

Web Site(s):

---

http://www.legopolis.com/minifig/index.html

Time Required:

- 45 minutes

Teaching the Lesson:

- As with all Web pages, be certain that you preview this one so that you ensure your browser and other software are compatible with this Web site. In addition, this page can take a long time to load, so be sure to start early.

- The minifigs can take on all sorts of interesting characteristics—you may need to look carefully to make sure they are appropriate for your class.

- Stories can be read to the class, and students can compare to see if they created similar minifigs.

- Drawing minifigs as story illustrations is a good optional activity.

Name: _____ Date: _____

Minifig Story

A "minifig" is a small toy person who lives in a world of Lego® toys. On this Web page, you can design your own "minifig" people, using different clothes, faces, and bodies.

Go to:

_____

http://www.legopolis.com/minifig/index.html

_____

While you wait for the page to load, get ready for your assignment: a story! You will choose and design at least four different minifigs. Write a story that includes each minifig. If you designed a minifig pirate, the story should be about pirates. For extra credit, you can draw pictures of your minifigs on the back of this page.

Title:

_____

Story:

_____

_____

_____

_____

_____

_____

_____

_____

_____

_____

Error File

Teacher Notes

Objectives:

Students will

- locate commonly misspelled or misused words.
- correct spelling and usage of words.

Materials Required:

- computer with Internet access
- pencil or pen

Web Site(s):

http://www.wsu.edu:8080/~brians/errors/errors.html

Time Required:

- 25 minutes

Teaching the Lesson:

- This lesson can easily be expanded for more advanced students to move toward the more complex words on the Web site list.

- Use this as an opportunity to explain why computer programs that check spelling do not allow students to skip proofreading papers before handing them in. This is because many spell checking programs do not correct accurately for usage errors, only spelling mistakes.

- If students have trouble generating their own list of commonly misspelled words, supply them with an example or two.

Name: _____ Date: _____

Error File

Everyone makes mistakes when writing or speaking. This Web site will help you find out some common errors made in the English language.

Go to:

http://www.wsu.edu:8080/~brians/errors/errors.html

Look up the incorrect words on the list below. Click on them and then write down the correct spelling or use of the word.

Incorrect word	Correct word
alot	_____
alright	_____
realtor	_____
expresso	_____
everyday	_____

Now pick five different words from the Web site list that you have spelled incorrectly or used the wrong way in the past. Write the word and then the corrected word or words as you did above.

Incorrect word	Correct word
_____	_____
_____	_____
_____	_____
_____	_____
_____	_____

Wow! Interjections!

Teacher Notes

Objectives:

Students will

- identify characteristics of interjections by listening to a song and following the lyrics.
- write sentences that contain interjections.

Materials Required:

- computer with Internet access
- pencil or pen

Web Site(s):

http://genxtvland.simplenet.com/SchoolHouseRock/song.hts?lo+interjections

Time Required:

- 35 minutes

Teaching the Lesson:

- Be sure to instruct the students about how to click the correct song link. This depends on which one(s) your Internet browser is compatible with. To find out which one works best, test it before the lesson.
- These songs may be familiar to you if you watched Saturday morning cartoons in the 1970s.
- If you or your students are of a musical bent, don't hesitate to have the students sing these songs as a group.

Name: _____ Date: _____

Wow! Interjections!

You use parts of speech called interjections all of the time. This Web site will help you become an interjection expert.

Whoops!
Ouch!
Hey!

Go to:

http://genxtvland.simplenet.com/SchoolHouseRock/song.hts?lo+interjections

Your teacher will tell you which link to click when you want to hear the song. Play the song and follow the lyrics on your screen. Then write down eight interjections below that are not used in the song.

After writing the interjection, use it in a sentence. Then you will be finished. Hooray!

Interjection	Sentence
_____	_____
_____	_____
_____	_____
_____	_____
_____	_____
_____	_____
_____	_____
_____	_____

Person, Place, or Thing?

Teacher Notes

Objectives:

Students will

- listen to a song about nouns and determine their characteristics.

- create sentences containing nouns.

Materials Required:

- computer with Internet access

- pencil or pen

Web Site(s):

---

http://genxtvland.simplenet.com/SchoolHouseRock/song.hts?lo+noun

---

Time Required:

- 20–25 minutes

Teaching the Lesson:

- Be sure the students are looking at the words as they listen to the song. You can quiz them along the way to check their understanding.

- If necessary, help them to generate a list of nouns on the board if they have difficulty making one themselves.

Name: _____ Date: _____

Person, Place, or Thing?

Nouns are parts of speech that you use when you mention any person, place, or thing. For another look at nouns and to hear a great song about them,

Go to:

http://genxtvland.simplenet.com/SchoolHouseRock/song.hts?lo+noun

Your teacher will tell you which link to click so you can hear the song. When you play the song, read the words and become a noun expert

Write 10 examples of nouns that are not used in the song. Then write a sentence for each.

Noun	Sentence
_____	_____
_____	_____
_____	_____
_____	_____
_____	_____
_____	_____
_____	_____
_____	_____
_____	_____
_____	_____

Flashy Flash Cards

Teacher Notes

Objectives:

Students will

- solve grade-appropriate math problems online.
- create flash cards to use for simple math operations.

Materials Required:

- computer with Internet access
- pencil or pen
- index cards or construction paper

Web Site(s):

http://www.wwinfo.com/jmi-bin/uncgi.cgi/math.tcl

Time Required:

- 35–40 minutes

Teaching the Lesson:

- Be sure to preview the online problems so you can help students choose the ones most appropriate to their skill levels.
- As an added challenge, have students move to a higher level or change the type of problem to one more complex.
- Students should make flash cards and quiz each other on the problems they chose. They should take care to make sure that the answers on the flash cards are correct!

$17 + 78 =$

$59 \div 13 =$

$12 \times 124 =$

Name: _____ Date: _____

Flashy Flash Cards

See how far you can go! Begin answering math questions by choosing the type of math (your teacher will help you with this part), complexity, and number size.

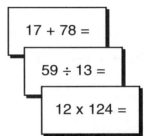

Go to:

http://www.wwinfo.com/jmi-bin/uncgi.cgi/math.tcl

Next, make your own flash cards! Trade with your partner when you have finished making ten cards. Each group of cards should be the same kind of problem. Do a group of addition, one of subtraction, and so on.

$? \div ? = ?$

$? - ? = ?$

$? \times ? = ?$

$? + ?$

$? \times ? = ?$

$- ? = ?$

$? - ? = ?$

$? \div ? = ?$

$? + ?$

$? \div ? =$

$? \times ? =$

$? + ? = ?$

$? \div ?$

$? + ? = ?$

$? \times ? =$

Checkers Check In

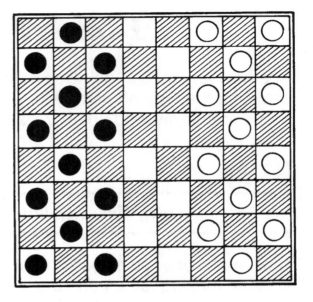

Teacher Notes

Additional Content Area(s):

- social studies
- language arts

Objectives:

Students will

- learn the rules of checkers.
- write down instructions on how to play checkers.

Materials Required:

- computer with Internet access
- pencil or pen
- construction paper (optional)
- colored markers/crayons(optional)

Web Site(s):

http://www.learn2.com/

Time Required:

- 35–50 minutes

Teaching the Lesson:

- This lesson is an excellent example of the "teaching as learning" strategy, where a student is asked to teach about a topic and learns it by doing so.
- It is most important that the students provide enough information in their explanations of the rules of checkers to be able to actually play the game. This is the best way to evaluate the quality of their work.
- As an optional activity, have students construct checkerboards and pieces as per the instructions on the Web page. Then let them play!

Name: _____ Date: _____

Checkers Check In

Checkers is a very old game that is still very popular all over the world. If you have played before, you already know how much fun it can be. If you are new to checkers, here is your chance to become an expert. Get ready to play.

Go to:

_____

http://www.learn2.com/

_____

Read the instructions and rules of how to play. Use the "back" button on your browser to return to the first page. Then answer the questions below.

1. How many squares are on a checkerboard?

   _____

2. What is it called when you take someone else's piece?

   _____

3. Pretend you are going to teach a friend how to play checkers. Write down in your own words the directions on how to play and the rules of the game. Then try the real thing using your own instructions.

How to Play Checkers

_____

_____

_____

_____

_____

_____

_____

Behind Bars

Teacher Notes

Objectives:

Students will

- correctly match faces of "criminals" in a concentration-style game to avoid letting them out of "prison."

- solve addition and subtraction word problems.

Materials Required:

- computer with Internet access
- pencil or pen

Web Site(s):

http://www.cyberkids.com/Games/lockdown/start.html

Time Required:

- 25–30 minutes

Teaching the Lesson:

- This activity is a variation of a concentration-style game.

- Be sure the students read the story (or read it together by making a handout) behind the characters and the idea behind the game.

- The follow-up questions are simple enough for all learning levels to take part.

Name: _____ Date: _____

Behind Bars

You're an assistant bounty hunter, and your job is to put the bad guys behind bars. And when they are in jail, you want to make sure they stay there.

Go to:

http://www.cyberkids.com/Games/lockdown/start.html

Fill in the information and click "play it." Read the story by clicking "story."

1. Your partner Wendall holds two jobs. What are they?

   _____

2. What happens each time that you mismatch your criminals in the game?

   _____

Use your back button and click "play."

3. After you finished, what was your score? How many criminals escaped?

   _____

4. Look carefully at the screen. How many jail cells are there?

   _____

5. If half of the criminals escaped, how many would be left?

   _____

6. How many of the criminals are wearing hats?

   _____

7. How many of the criminals are not wearing hats?

   _____

8. How much money did you and your partner Wendall earn for this job?

   _____

9. If you decided to give half of your money to Wendall, how much would you have left?

   _____

Same or Similar?

Teacher Notes

Objectives:

Students will

- observe and recognize patterns among various pictures.
- draw their own similar/same pictures.

Materials Required:

- computer with Internet access
- pencil or pen
- colored pens/pencils/crayons

Web Site(s):

---

http://pathfinder.com/travel/klutz/contents_which.html

Time Required:

- 25–35 minutes

Teaching the Lesson:

- Students will have to observe carefully to see the pattern differences in this activity. The most difficult part may be to write down an explanation of why the objects are similar or different—they may need you to help them on the first one.

- It is important that students try to keep their own drawings simple so they can be accurate when drawing slight pattern differences.

Name: _____ Date: _____

Same or Similar?

When something is similar to another thing, it means they are a close match but not quite the same. Are you good at observing things? Can you see small details in a picture?

Go to:

http://pathfinder.com/travel/klutz/contents_which.html

Your job will be to find out how pictures that look the same at first may not be.

Begin with a look at the *four boys* link.
  1. Which two were the same?

  _____

  2. Why were they the same but different from the others?

  _____

Next look at the *six fish* link.
  3. Which two were the same?

  _____

  4. Why were they the same but different from the others?

  _____

Next are the *nine cows*. Click on the link.
  5. Which two were the same?

  _____

  6. Why were they the same but different from the others?

  _____

In the space below, draw your own pictures of four similar objects where only two are the same. Try to see if your neighbor can tell them apart!

_____

_____

_____

Your Own Personal Fortuneteller

Teacher Notes

Objectives:

Students will

- construct a folding "crystal ball" out of paper.
- create different "fortunes" for the crystal ball.

Materials Required:

- computer with Internet access
- pencil or pen
- colored pencils/pens/crayons
- sheet of blank, white paper

Web Site(s):

---

http://pathfinder.com/travel/klutz/fortune.html

Time Required:

- 45 minutes

Teaching the Lesson:

- This device has been around for many years. It is fun for any grade or ability level. Some students will require help constructing the device, using the directions on the Web site.

- You may want to look at their list of fortunes before students write them on the device to be sure they are appropriate for school.

Name: _____ Date: _____

Your Own Personal Fortuneteller

Have you ever heard of a crystal ball? Some people who call themselves fortunetellers use these tools to "see" the future. In this activity, you will make your own fortunetelling tool—a paper crystal ball.

Go to:

---

http://pathfinder.com/travel/klutz/fortune.html

Carefully follow the directions on how to fold the paper into a "crystal ball." Be sure you color each of the eight triangles a different color. Then you will need to write a "fortune" under each one for a person to look at.

After you build the paper crystal ball, write down the eight fortunes you have chosen below. Then try the fortuneteller on your friends—will any of them come true?

Triangle Number	Fortune
1.	_____
2.	_____
3.	_____
4.	_____
5.	_____
6.	_____
7.	_____
8.	_____

Pitch Me a Question!

Teacher Notes

Objectives:

Students will

- solve math problems in a baseball-style game.
- record their scores during the game.

Materials Required:

- computer with Internet access
- pencil or pen

Web Site(s):

http://www.funbrain.com/math/index.html

Time Required:

- 25–30 minutes

Teaching the Lesson:

- You will need to help students select the most appropriate level of questions. This game can be extended and replayed as students improve their math skills.
- Playing in teams is an option that allows for a more baseball-like game play.
- Be sure they fill out their score cards accurately on the students' work sheets.

Name: _____ Date: _____

Pitch Me a Question!

In this activity you will be playing a game of "baseball" with math questions that the computer pitches to you.

Go to:

http://www.funbrain.com/math/index.html

Choose the level and the kind of game (your teacher may help you with this).

Remember, the game is over if you get three outs. See if you can score higher than your friends or play as a team! Play at least three games and fill in the scoreboard below as you play.

Baseball Scorecard

Game #1

Player Name	Hits	Runs	Outs	Score
_____	_____	_____	_____	_____
_____	_____	_____	_____	_____

Game #2

Player Name	Hits	Runs	Outs	Score
_____	_____	_____	_____	_____
_____	_____	_____	_____	_____

Game #3

Player Name	Hits	Runs	Outs	Score
_____	_____	_____	_____	_____
_____	_____	_____	_____	_____

Cash It In!

Teacher Notes

Objectives:

Students will

- add and subtract coins.

- determine coin combinations.

Materials Required:

- computer with Internet access

- pencil or pen

Web Site(s):

http://www.funbrain.com/cashreg/index.html

Time Required:

- 35–40 minutes

Teaching the Lesson:

- Be sure students understand how to fill in the chart. They should fill it in just as it appears on the Web site, one for each question.

- For a hands-on extension, use real coins as a follow-up.

- You will need to assist students in choosing the appropriate level to play.

Name: _____ Date: _____

Cash It In!

Do have any change in your pocket? Are you good at keeping track of it?

This game will help you practice your money skills—so be careful and cash in!

Go to:

http://www.funbrain.com/cashreg/index.html

Your teacher will help you decide on the level to play. Then press start. Write down each question, using the chart below. Fill in the answers on your computer and on this paper. Do at least fifteen questions.

Amount of Sale	Amount Paid	Coins You Will Get Back			
		Pennies	*Nickels*	*Dimes*	*Quarters*
1. _____	_____	_____	_____	_____	_____
2. _____	_____	_____	_____	_____	_____
3. _____	_____	_____	_____	_____	_____
4. _____	_____	_____	_____	_____	_____
5. _____	_____	_____	_____	_____	_____
6. _____	_____	_____	_____	_____	_____
7. _____	_____	_____	_____	_____	_____
8. _____	_____	_____	_____	_____	_____
9. _____	_____	_____	_____	_____	_____
10. _____	_____	_____	_____	_____	_____
11. _____	_____	_____	_____	_____	_____
12. _____	_____	_____	_____	_____	_____
13. _____	_____	_____	_____	_____	_____
14. _____	_____	_____	_____	_____	_____
15. _____	_____	_____	_____	_____	_____

Froggy Math

Teacher Notes

Objectives:

Students will

- solve a variety of addition and subtraction problems.
- solve word problems.

Materials Required:

- computer with Internet access
- pencil or pen

Web Site(s):

http://www.adventure.com/kids/games/frogwell/

Time Required:

- 40 minutes

Teaching the Lesson:

- Students may need help "catching" the correct solutions to the math problems presented.
- They should keep track of their cumulative points as they play.
- Lower-level students may need help with the word problems on the student page. Team them up with other students as necessary.

Name: _____ Date: _____

Froggy Math

Did you know that frogs use their tongues to catch insects? You already knew that, didn't you? Well, now you are going to see that this special frog can use its tongue to catch numbers, too.

Go to:

http://www.adventure.com/kids/games/frogwell/

Your job is to click the space bar when the correct answer to the math problem appears close-by—catching it! You need to reach a score of 500 points to win.

Your Score: _____

Bonus Questions:

1. If a frog could eat 3 flies in one minute, how many flies could it eat in 5 minutes?

   _____

   _____

2. If eating one worm is like eating 5 flies, how many worms would a frog have to eat to take the place of 3 worms?

   _____

   _____

3. If a frog's tongue is 6 inches long and the fly it shoots at is 4 inches (10.16 cm) away, how much tongue does the frog have to spare?

   _____

   _____

4. Suppose a frog weighs 55 grams. Without its tongue the frog would weigh 49 grams. How much does the frog's tongue weigh?

   _____

   _____

   _____

Slide, Don't Slip!

Teacher Notes

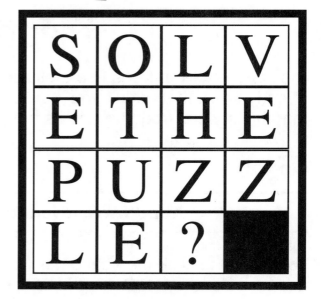

Objectives:

Students will

- solve three slider-type puzzles.
- draw the solutions to each puzzle.

Materials Required:

- computer with Internet access
- pencil or pen

Web Site(s):

http://www.adventure.com/kids/slider/?1

Time Required:

- 35–40 minutes

Teaching the Lesson:

- There are many puzzles available as an extension for students who finish early.
- Drawing the puzzle solution ensures that students have actually solved it. You may even have students divide the solutions into square sections that reflect the puzzle pieces.
- Be sure students feel comfortable manipulating the puzzle pieces online.

Name: _____ Date: _____

Slide, Don't Slip!

This Web page has several puzzles for you to solve. Move the tiles by clicking on the one you want to move to the blank space. Make a picture for each puzzle. Then draw the picture after you solve each one.

S	O	L	V
E	T	H	E
P	U	Z	Z
L	E	?	■

Go to:

http://www.adventure.com/kids/slider/?1

Drawing One

Drawing Two

Drawing Three

Math Dot Connections

Teacher Notes

Objectives:

Students will

- connect dots between numbers.
- draw solutions to the puzzles.

Materials Required:

- computer with Internet access
- pencil or pen

Web Site(s):

http://www.adventure.com/kids/connect_dots/index.cgi

Time Required:

- 30 minutes

Teaching the Lesson:

- This activity is best applied to lower-level students.
- Drawings should only be required to be as accurate as is reasonable for this level of student.
- As an extension, have students each write a short story about each figure they create.

Name: _____ Date: _____

Math Dot Connections

You can make pictures by connecting dots on these Web pages. After you finish connecting all the dots, write down what you have made and then draw it.

Go to:

http://www.adventure.com/kids/connect_dots/index.cgi

Connect-the-dots number one: Name _____	Connect-the-dots number two: Name _____
Connect-the-dots number three: Name _____	Connect-the-dots number four: Name _____

Know Your History

Teacher Notes

Objectives:

Students will

- read and answer questions regarding important African Americans.

- research online for further information about a famous African American of their own choosing.

Materials Required:

- computer with Internet access

- pencil or pen

Web Site(s):

http://www.afroam.org/children/brain/historyquiz/q1.html

http://www.yahoo.com

Time Required:

- 35–40 minutes

Teaching the Lesson:

- This lesson is appropriate during any part of the year, but during Black History Month is a good time to discuss the contributions of African Americans to our society.

- Students may need help deciphering the information they obtain during their research. Don't let them get overwhelmed. Help them focus on just a few aspects of the person who interests them the most.

- There are many possible extensions to this activity, including classroom presentations, plays, and further research on this topic online.

Name: _____ Date: _____

Know Your History

Answer the questions about African-American history, using the clues given at the Web site below. Write down the correct answer to each question.

Go to:

http://www.afroam.org/children/brain/historyquiz/q1.html

Choose **two** people from the list of correct answers to the quiz.

1. _____

2. _____

Go to:

http://www.yahoo.com

Type in one person's name and find out at least five facts about this person, using other Internet Web sites. Write down those facts below. Then do the same thing with the other person you chose and write down those facts below. Use of the back of this sheet if you need more space.

_____

_____

_____

_____

_____

_____

_____

Mysterious Stonehenge

Teacher Notes

Objectives:

Students will

- explore the myths and structure of Stonehenge.

- record information about Stonehenge.

- research the Internet for other mysterious structures.

Materials Required:

- computer with Internet access

- pencil or pen

Web Site(s):

http://witcombe.bcpw.sbc.edu/EMStonehenge.html

Time Required:

- 35 minutes

Teaching the Lesson:

- Have an introductory discussion of ancient mysteries such as the pyramids, etc., with the students. Use Stonehenge as just one example of these. Then bring them online after they learn some background.

- An extension of this is to create a small model of Stonehenge, either in its present state or its purported "original" state.

- Students could write a story about Stonehenge or another mysterious place that has remained for centuries and beyond. They could also create a play depicting scenes from its past as it changed over time.

Name: _____   Date: _____

Mysterious Stonehenge

Perhaps you have seen pictures of one of the earth's strangest mysteries, Stonehenge. Thousands of years old, this amazing structure built of huge stones brings people from around the world to try to find out its hidden secrets. On the Web page you will go to, some of these secrets have been revealed.

Go to:

http://witcombe.bcpw.sbc.edu/EMStonehenge.html

1. In what country is Stonehenge located?

   _____

2. What are sarsens?

   _____

3. What do you think megalithic means?

   _____

4. Is the true purpose of Stonehenge known today?

   _____

5. Do you think any of today's modern buildings will remain standing for thousands of years like Stonehenge? Why or why not?

   _____

6. Think of at least one more ancient mystery other than Stonehenge. Write down everything you know about it and then do an Internet search to find out more! Use the following search engine to help you.

http://www.altavista.digital.com

_____

_____

Save the World—With Geography!

Teacher Notes

Objectives:

Students will

- apply knowledge of geography to "save the world."
- add their accumulated points.

Materials Required:

- computer with Internet access
- pencil or pen

Web Site(s):

http://www.eduplace.com/geo/indexhi.html

Time Required:

- 35–40 minutes

Teaching the Lesson:

- Students should work in teams of two or three during this activity.
- You can decide in advance which part of the U.S. geography you wish to concentrate on, or you can use the entire country.
- A brief primer on the location of different states is a good idea before beginning. This also makes a good culminating activity for a U.S. geography unit.

Name: _____ Date: _____

Save the World—With Geography!

Did you ever think that knowing your gerography can help you save the world? Well, it can, in more ways than one. Get ready to spin the globe.

Go to:

http://www.eduplace.com/geo/indexhi.html

To find out how you can "save the world," click on the "Orbit and the alien threat" link. After you have finished, write two or three sentences explaining how knowing geography will help you "save the world."

_____

_____

_____

_____

Use your back button to return to the page with the map of the world. Click on any link, choosing the Northeast, South, or the United States to begin the game.

Your teacher will help you decide on a category to work on. Click on that category and write down your answer to each question in the space below. After you write down the answer, click "submit choice" to see if you were right! Add up the points you earn in each category. Try to earn more points than the other teams in your class!

_____

_____

_____

_____

Safe Surfing

Teacher Notes

Objectives:

Students will

- explore rules of safe Internet behavior.
- write and share rules of safe Internet behavior.

Materials Required:

- computer with Internet access
- pencil or pen
- poster board/construction paper and related materials (optional)

Web Site(s):

http://kidscom.com/orakc/Games/newSafe/

Time Required:

- 25–60 minutes

Teaching the Lesson:

- A good optional activity is for students to make posters involving these rules and perhaps hang them in the computer lab or another appropriate area on campus.
- Be sure to model these safe behaviors yourself, or students will not take them seriously.
- Discuss other rules of Internet safety that the students create.

Name: _____ Date: _____

Safe Surfing

The Internet is a great place to surf through cyberspace. Just like any activity, there are some things you need to be careful to watch out for. Even when you cross the street, you need to watch out for cars. On the Internet, you need to watch out and play it smart, too.

Go to:

http://kidscom.com/orakc/Games/newSafe/

Read the Internet safety tips on this Web page. Imagine yourself following each tip each time you log on, whether you are at home or at school. Then at the bottom of the page, click on the "just play" link to see what you remember.

Write the sentence you create for each question.

1. _____

2. _____

3. _____

4. _____

5. _____

6. _____

7. _____

8. _____

9. _____

10. _____

Where Is That Volcano, Anyway?

Teacher Notes

Objective:

Students will

- identify the states in which various volcanoes are located.

Materials Required:

- computer with Internet access
- pencil or pen

Web Site(s):

http://volcano.und.nodak.edu/vwdocs/kids/fun/usa_matching/Matching.html

Time Required:

- 40 minutes

Teaching the Lesson:

- This activity should be an integral part of a volcano-related unit. Students may be surprised to find volcanoes in or near their own state.
- You can also extend this activity into a history lesson on volcanoes in the past and the damage and loss of life they have caused.

Name: _____ Date: _____

Where Is That Volcano, Anyway?

Many states in the U.S. have volcanoes. Most of them are not considered to be "active," meaning that they have not erupted in many years. Do you have any volcanoes in your state?

Go to:

http://volcano.und.nodak.edu/vwdocs/kids/fun/usa_matching/Matching.html

Follow the directions on the Web page after it loads. Write down the name of each of the eighteen volcanoes on the map and the state that it can be found in.

Name of Volcano	Found in What State?
1. _____	_____
2. _____	_____
3. _____	_____
4. _____	_____
5. _____	_____
6. _____	_____
7. _____	_____
8. _____	_____
9. _____	_____
10. _____	_____
11. _____	_____
12. _____	_____
13. _____	_____
14. _____	_____
15. _____	_____
16. _____	_____
17. _____	_____
18. _____	_____

White House Tour with the First Cat

Teacher Notes

Objectives:

Students will

- explore the history of the White House.
- answer questions about present and previous White House residents.

Materials Required:

- computer with Internet access
- pencil or pen

Web Site(s):

http://www.whitehouse.gov/WH/kids/html/home.html

Time Required:

- 40 minutes

Teaching the Lesson:

- This activity provides an opportunity for as much or as little exploration into the topic as is appropriate.
- Advanced students should explore the links that move into history of the White House.
- Students with a lower reading level should work in teams and stay with the "tour" more closely.

Name: _____ Date: _____

White House Tour with the First Cat

What would it be like to visit the house of the president of the United States? The best "person" to ask might be one who lives there—like Socks, the official cat of the White House!

Go to:

---

http://www.whitehouse.gov/WH/kids/html/home.html

Go to each numbered link to find out all sorts of things about where the president lives, kids in the White House, and their pets! Then answer the questions below.

1. What is the address of the White House?

   _____

2. Did George Washington ever live in the White House?

   _____

3. Bill Clinton is the (circle the correct answer) 40th, 45th, 42nd, 50th president of the United States.

4. Who is the first child to live in the White House since Amy Carter?

   _____

5. What was the name of President Abraham Lincoln's youngest son?

   _____

6. President Clinton has two pets. What kinds of animals are they?

   _____

7. Which president had a pet goat?

   _____

8. President Bush's dog did something no other First Pet has ever done. What did she do?

   _____

How do you think a First Pet like Socks spends its day? Write down three or four things you think that a First Pet does that regular pets might not do during the day. Use the back of this sheet to write your answer.

State of the States

Teacher Notes

Objectives:

Students will

- identify and record state capitals.
- identify and record state nicknames.

Materials Required:

- computer with Internet access
- pencil or pen

Web Site(s):

http://www.50states.com/

Time Required:

- 40 minutes

Teaching the Lesson:

- Be sure that students look for the nickname or phrase that goes with each state. A state may be nicknamed "the buckeye state" while another may have a saying such as "land of 10,000 lakes."
- Advanced students can do more than the twelve states required on the work sheet.
- An extension of this activity is to explore the meanings and origins of the nicknames or phrases that go with each state.

Name: _____ Date: _____

State of the States

Do you know the capital of your state? How about the capitals of three more states? Did you know each state has a nickname or special saying that goes with it? Here is your chance to see the capitals and nicknames of all 50 states!

Go to:

http://www.50states.com/

Find your own state on the list. Click on it and then write down the information below.

Name of My State   **Nickname or Saying**

_____   _____

Now do the same for 12 more states.

_____   _____

_____   _____

_____   _____

_____   _____

_____   _____

_____   _____

_____   _____

_____   _____

_____   _____

_____   _____

_____   _____

_____   _____

To Betsy's House to Make a Flag

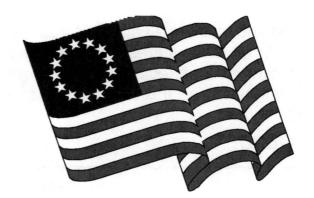

Teacher Notes

Objectives:

Students will

- examine the history of the U.S. flag.
- record the meaning of the flag and the important persons who designed it.

Materials Required:

- computer with Internet access
- pencil or pen
- colored pencils, pens, or crayons

Web Site(s):

http://www.ushistory.org/betsy/flagtale.html

http://www.ushistory.org/betsy/flagtriv.html

Time Required:

- 35–40 minutes

Teaching the Lesson:

- The reading level in this activity can be challenging to lower-level students. Pair them with another student as they go through this activity.
- As an extension, students can explore the wide variety of flags used by the colonists and their meanings, as well as drawing them.
- Making posters of the different flags is another good extension if time permits.
- A play re-enacting the discussion of the flag with Betsy Ross is another good activity for advanced students.

Name: _____ Date: _____

To Betsy's House to Make a Flag

Many people know that a woman named Betsy Ross sewed the first American flag. But there is much more to the story of the flag of our country than that!

Go to:

http://www.ushistory.org/betsy/flagtale.html

Draw a picture of the first American flag as Betsy Ross sewed it.

1. Who were the three people who met with Betsy Ross and asked her to sew the flag?

   _____

2. One of the other flags used was known as the "rattlesnake" flag. What did the rattlesnake flag mean?

   _____

Go to:

http://www.ushistory.org/betsy/flagtriv.html

3. Who cut the flag into pieces and was honored for it?

   _____

4. What does it mean when someone flies the flag upside down?

   _____

5. Who was "Shipwreck" Kelly?

   _____

Zoom In on Africa!

Teacher Notes

Objectives:

Students will

- explore African animals.
- write a message in ancient Nubian language.
- list the names of the countries in Africa.

Materials Required:

- computer with Internet access
- pencil or pen

Web Site(s):

http://www.ZoomSchool.com/

http://www.EnchantedLearning.com/cgi-bin/Africa/

http://www.africaonline.com/AfricaOnline/kidsonly/games/crossword.html

Time Required:

- 45 minutes

Teaching the Lesson:

- This lesson is ideal as part of an introduction to a study on Africa. It allows the students to see the variety of peoples, countries, animals, and traditions there.

- Advanced students can explore as far as they wish, and some of the links provide daily news from various areas of the continent.

- The ancient Nubian pictographs are used to create a secret message. Students may need help drawing these. Remind them to keep messages simple!

Name: _____ Date: _____

Zoom In on Africa!

Africa is a large continent with many different countries. It is a land of many different languages and customs among its people. You will find the most amazing animals on earth there as well. Lets take a closer look!

Go to:

http://www.ZoomSchool.com/

Click on the link to African animals. Write three things about the animal described.

1. _____
2. _____
3. _____

Can you decode the language of the ancient Nubians?

Go to:

http://www.EnchantedLearning.com/school/Africa/

http://www.africaonline.com/AfricaOnline/kidsonly/games/crossword.html

Look carefully at the symbols for each letter in the alphabet. Then decode each letter one by one. Write the message below.

_____

How many countries are there in Africa?

Go to:

http://www.lib.utexas.edu/Libs/PCL/Map_collection/africa/Africa_6_97.jpg

Look at all the countries of Africa. List them on the back of this sheet.

What's in the News?

Teacher Notes

Objectives:

Students will

- read and explore a current news story.
- write a summary of the news event.

Materials Required:

- computer with Internet access
- pencil or pen

Web Site(s):

http://www.morning.com/currentissue/currentissue.html

Time Required:

- 40–50 minutes

Teaching the Lesson:

- Be sure students choose topics they are interested in and feel are important before they write their summaries.
- They need to distinguish between the two parts of the writing assignment—explain it to them carefully and check their progress.
- Allow for some time to browse the different stories presented so they each can find one they enjoy reading.

Name: _____ Date: _____

What's in the News?

What kind of news is important to you? In this assignment, your job is to read about a news event on this Web page.

Go to:

http://www.morning.com/currentissue/currentissue.html

Choose any of the topics you wish and click on one to read more. Then use the space below to write a description about the news you just read. Next, explain why this news is important to you—and your classroom.

Title of news event I read:

_____

My news event was about

_____

_____

_____

_____

_____

I think this news event is important because

_____

_____

_____

_____

_____

_____

Your Name in Hieroglyphics

Teacher Notes

Objectives:

Students will

- use Egyptian hieroglyphics to write their names and messages.
- discuss the use of hieroglyphics in writing.

Materials Required:

- computer with Internet access
- pencil or pen

Web Site(s):

http://www.rom.on.ca/egypt/hiero/hiero.html

Time Required:

- 30 minutes

Teaching the Lesson:

- This is an ideal lesson to incorporate into a study of ancient cultures.
- Students will need to draw the symbols carefully so their neighbors can decipher their secret messages.
- Lower-level students may need to be paired with others in order to complete the assignment successfully.
- Place your own secret message on the board for them all to solve together as an introduction or a final activity.

Name: _____ Date: _____

Your Name in Hieroglyphics

Hieroglyphics is an ancient alphabet made up of pictures instead of letters. The most famous hieroglyphics are Egyptian.

Go to:

http://www.rom.on.ca/egypt/hiero/hiero.html

Study the hieroglyphics. What letter does each hieroglyph stand for? Then write your name below, using hieroglyphics.

Your Name (in English) _____

Your Name (in hieroglyphics) _____

Which language is easier to write? Explain your answer.

_____

_____

Now write a one-sentence-long secret message using hieroglyphics. Pass this paper to your neighbor and have him or her write down what your message is!

Secret Message (in hieroglyphics)

Secret Message (in English)

_____

Chocolate from Bean to Bar

Teacher Notes

Objectives:

Students will

- explore the process of making chocolate.
- identify the materials and stages of making chocolate.

Materials Required:

- computer with Internet access
- pencil or pen
- chocolate candy (optional)

Web Site(s):

http://www.hersheys.com/hershey/tour/plant.index.html

Time Required:

- 25 minutes

Teaching the Lesson:

- This answers one of the many "How do they do that?" questions kids often wonder about. Use this activity as a launchpad to study South America, the rain forest, agriculture, and economics.

- You may want to bring in some unsweetened baker's chocolate and have the students identify which process has not occurred in order to make it.

- In addition, giving students a small chocolate sample would be a good way for them to appreciate the intricacies of chocolate production. Be sure to check with parents for food allergies before doing this.

Name: _____ Date: _____

Chocolate from Bean to Bar

Chances are that you like chocolate. Most people do.
Even if you don't like chocolate, did you ever wonder where
it comes from? Here is the best place to find out!

Go to:

---

http://www.hersheys.com/hershey/tour/plant.index.html

---

1. If you were to eat a cacao bean, how would it taste?

   _____

2. How do they make the sugar used in chocolate?

   _____

3. Almonds are grown in what state? Where do peanuts come from?

   _____

4. How does the milk get from the farmer to the chocolate factory?

   _____

5. Why do you think beans from different countries taste different?

   _____

6. What are "nibs?"

   _____

7. What is the one ingredient that is used in all the chocolate at the factory?

   _____

8. If you were to eat "crumb," what would it taste like?

   _____

9. How long does "conching" take?

   _____

10. What is put into a "mould?"

    _____

Candy Science!

Teacher Notes

Additional Content Area(s):

- art

Objectives:

Students will

- create colors.
- identify melting points of three substances.
- determine the pH of common substances.
- determine frictional forces of three different materials.

Materials Required:

- computer with Internet access
- pencil or pen

Web Site(s):

---

http://www.wonka.com/InventionRoom/game_world.html

Time Required:

- 40 minutes

Teaching the Lesson:

- This lesson includes several key concepts in physical science that are made exceptionally easy to understand. Review these concepts yourself to make sure you can answer student questions.

- These are good introductions to in-class laboratory assignments involving any or all of the four major concepts presented: color, melting points, pH, and frictional forces.

Name: _____ Date: _____

Candy Science!

Time for some science in the secret laboratory!

Go to:

---

http://www.wonka.com/InventionRoom/game_world.html

Click on the numbered links in order, starting with number one. Answer all of the questions below.

1. What colors do you use to make purple?

   _____

2. What colors do you use to make orange?

   _____

3. What does "melting point" mean?

   _____

4. What is the melting point of sugar?

   _____

5. What is the melting point of ice?

   _____

6. What do scientists use the pH scale for?

   _____

7. Is soap an acid or a base?

   _____

8. Is cola an acid or a base?

   _____

9. Are sour tasting foods usually acids or bases?

   _____

10. Which has the most friction, oil, water, or sand?

    _____

Red Planet

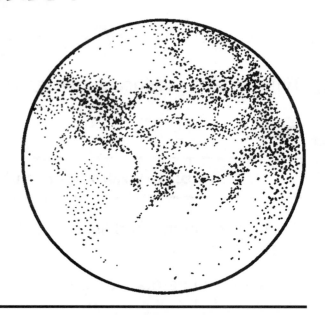

Teacher Notes

Objective:

Students will

- write facts about the solar system and Mars in particular.

Materials Required:

- computer with Internet access
- pencil or pen

Web Site(s):

http://craton.geol.brocku.ca/faculty/ff/nineplanets/mars.html

Time Required:

- 25–35 minutes

Teaching the Lesson:

- Students would be best served if they did some preliminary work on the solar system before beginning this activity.
- This page may take a while to load, so be prepared.

Name: _____   Date: _____

Red Planet

Your mission: learn about the red planet, Mars.

Go to:

http://craton.geol.brocku.ca/faculty/ff/nineplanets/mars.html

Answer the following questions.

1. How far is Mars from the Sun? _____

    _____

2. What other name is Mars sometimes called? _____

    _____

3 How long has Mars been known? _____

    _____

4. When did the first spacecraft visit Mars? When was the last time a Mars lander landed successfully on Mars?

    _____

5. How is the climate on Mars? _____

    _____

6. What does Mars have at both poles? _____

    _____

Watch Your Local Birds

Teacher Notes

Objectives:

Students will

- explore the hobby of bird watching.
- determine habits of different bird types.

Materials Required:

- computer with Internet access
- pencil or pen
- drawing supplies (optional)

Web Site(s):

http://www.enchantedlearning.com/subjects/birds/Birdwatching.html

Time Required:

- 40 minutes

Teaching the Lesson:

- This is an ideal lesson to do in the spring or early fall when birds are nearby.
- There are many extensions from this activity, including specific bird studies, building a birdhouse or feeder in class, and studying endangered species.
- Be sure to let advanced students explore the links on this page, and gifted students can do additional work using these resources.

Name: _____ Date: _____

Watch Your Local Birds

Watching birds is a fascinating and challenging hobby. You can learn a lot and must know a lot to find birds and see how they behave. Chances are that you have birds that live near you or your school. Now you can learn how to watch them up close.

Go to:

http://www.enchantedlearning.com/subjects/birds/Birdwatching.html

Read the information about bird watching. If you wish, you can click on the links to find out more about each topic. Then answer the questions below. Use the back button on your browser to return to the first page.

1. What are three examples of bird categories?

_____

2. Name a bird in each of the categories you named above.

_____

3. Why are bushes and dense hedges valuable to birds?

_____

4. What kinds of birds are attracted to flowers?

_____

5. What are three kinds of birds you can attract using a birdhouse?

_____

6. How can you make a simple bird feeder at home?

_____

7. What ingredient should NOT be used when making "nectar"?

_____

8. Where do hummingbirds usually get nectar from?

_____

Bonus: Click on the "Hummingbirds drink nectar" link. Then, on the back of this page, draw a picture of a hummingbird at a feeder drinking nectar or explain why a perch is important to have on a hummingbird feeder.

"Cyberian" Tiger

Teacher Notes

Objective:

Students will

- design a care and feeding program for an endangered Siberian tiger.

Materials Required:

- computer with Internet access
- pencil or pen

Web Site(s):

http://www.5tigers.org/talkback/talk.htm

Time Required:

- 25–30 minutes

Teaching the Lesson:

- A discussion of endangered species in general would be a good introduction. In addition, students can relate stories of their own pets to the class.
- If possible, schedule a field trip to a local zoo or museum (either real or virtual) to learn more about these and other endangered animals.
- There is also a Fun and Games section on this web site that students can go to as an extension activity for the lesson.

Name: _____ Date: _____

"Cyberian" Tiger

Do you have a pet? If you do, you know how much work it is to take care of a pet properly. Imagine having to care for an endangered animal—one of the few that remained in the world!

Go to:

http://www.5tigers.org/talkback/talk.htm

Click on each of the questions listed. Read the pages, follow the links and answer the following questions.

1. Where do tigers live? _____

_____

2. What do these places have in common?_____

_____

3. Why do tigers have stripes?_____

_____

4. How fast can a tiger run?_____

_____

5. Why doesn't a tiger chase its prey?_____

_____

6. Do tigers eat people?_____

_____

7. In India, what are the two solutions people have invented to protect themselves from being attacked by a tiger?

_____

_____

8. Can I tame a tiger to be my pet? _____

Volcanic Puzzles

Teacher Notes

Objectives:

Students will

- complete a sliding volcanic puzzle.
- determine their improvement when solving the puzzle again.

Materials Required:

- computer with Internet access
- pencil or pen
- drawing/coloring materials

Web Site(s):

http://volcano.und.nodak.edu/vwdocs/kids/fun/slider/SlideGame.html

Time Required:

- 20 minutes

Teaching the Lesson:

- Some students may need help operating the slider to move the puzzle pieces.
- This short activity is an especially good way to generate interest in volcanoes as a subject within your earth science curriculum.
- The puzzle records how long the student took to solve the puzzle. You can also use the follow-up questions to begin a discussion of why they improved their times after trying it again.

Name: _____ Date: _____

Volcanic Puzzles

You probably know that living near a volcano can be dangerous when it erupts. There are people all over the world who live near volcanoes anyway. If you live near a volcano, or even if you don't, you need to know what's up when they erupt!

Go to:

http://volcano.und.nodak.edu/vwdocs/kids/fun/slider/SlideGame.html

How long will it take you to complete the volcano puzzle? After the game loads on the screen, click the blank spot to move one piece at a time. Check your time against your neighbors! Record your time and then do the puzzle one more time. Did you complete it faster or slower the second time?

Time to Complete Puzzle (first time)   _____

Time to Complete Puzzle (second time)   _____

Difference Between First and Second Times _____

Better or Worse the Second Time?   _____

Draw a picture below of the Completed Puzzle to show that you finished it.

Be Safe with Electricity

Teacher Notes

Objective:

Students will

- examine and record important safety rules when using electricity.

Materials Required:

- computer with Internet access
- pencil or pen

Web Site(s):

http://www.miamisci.org/af/sln/frankenstein/safety.html

Time Required:

- 25 minutes

Teaching the Lesson:

- Students should be prompted to discuss the ways in which electricity is used at home. This will personalize the rules they write down during this activity.

- Some students may need help finding the "rule" in each explanation about the different electrical personalities on the Web site.

Name: _____ Date: _____

Be Safe with Electricity

Without electricity, our lives would be very different. But electricity can be a monster of a problem if you don't treat it carefully! Here's how to be safe when you use electricity.

Safety First!

Go to:

http://www.miamisci.org/af/sln/frankenstein/safety.html

When you see the picture of the house with all the monsters, click on one of them. Read the safety rule about electricity for each monster. Then write it down in the space below. Click on at least six different monsters.

Monster Name	**Safety Rule**
_____	_____
_____	_____
_____	_____
_____	_____
_____	_____
_____	_____

Write five things that you could not do if we did not have any electricity.

1. _____

2. _____

3. _____

4. _____

5. _____

A Common Disease

Teacher Notes

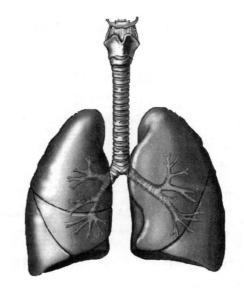

Objectives:

Students will

- examine the causes, symptoms, and treatments for asthma.

- answer questions pertaining to the above.

Materials Required:

- computer with Internet access

- pencil or pen

Web Site(s):

http://galen.med.virginia.edu/~smb4v/tutorials/asthma/asthma1.html

Time Required:

- 30–35 minutes

Teaching the Lesson:

- A class discussion about asthma prior to this activity is a good idea. You may want to survey the class to see how many people know someone with asthma. Be aware that some students may not want to publicize their own battles with asthma.

- As an extension to this activity, have students make posters or list things in the environment that may contribute to asthma attacks.

- You may need to assist some students with a few of the vocabulary words on this Web site.

Name: _____ Date: _____

A Common Disease

Chances are you know someone with asthma. Maybe you have asthma yourself. What exactly is asthma? Most people know that it has something to do with difficulty in breathing. The Web page you will visit next has lots of important information about this very common condition.

Go to:

http://galen.med.virginia.edu/~smb4v/tutorials/asthma/asthma1.html

Read the information on the Web page carefully. Click on any links to find out different things about asthma. Be sure you return to the original page by using the "back" button on your browser.

1. What body system is affected by asthma?

   _____

2. What would you notice about a person who is having an asthma attack?

   _____

Click on the pictures of the kids on the Web page to hear what it's like to have an asthma attack.

   _____

3. Why do you think having an asthma attack can be frightening?

   _____

Click on the link "How?"

4. Why do many people use inhalers when they have an asthma attack?

   _____

5. Write three things that you can do to help a person having an attack.

   _____

   _____

   _____

Safety First

Teacher Notes

Objectives:

Students will

- read about fire safety.
- determine and write about what can be done to be safe in the event of a fire.

Materials Required:

- computer with Internet access
- pencil or pen

Web Site(s):

http://www.uoknor.edu/oupd/kidsafe/fire.htm

Time Required:

- 20–25 minutes

Teaching the Lesson:

- If students drift too far into the Web site, they will end up in the Electrical Safety section—be sure they use the "back" button to stay on track.

- You should take this opportunity for a discussion of what can cause a fire, fire hazards in the home, and perhaps some statistics regarding children and fires to motivate them about this topic.

- This presents an opportunity to study behavior of fires and smoke in terms of a science unit on basic chemistry. Another opportunity might be to have the local fire department do a presentation and demonstration for your class.

- Have students help you locate fire safety equipment in your room and/or on school grounds.

Name: _____ Date: _____

Safety First

Read the information on the fire safety Web site. When you have finished reading each page, answer the questions below.

Go to:

http://www.uoknor.edu/oupd/kidsafe/fire.htm

1. If there is a fire, should you search for extra clothes and a jacket before leaving the house? Explain.

   _____

2. Should you ever try to fight a fire, even a small one?

   _____

3. Write down all the safety rules about fires. Which one do you think is the most important to you?

   _____

4. What should you do if your clothes catch on fire? How about if your friend's clothes catch fire?

   _____

5. Why is a fire escape plan important to have BEFORE you have a fire at home?

   _____

6. Write down two ways that you can get out of your bedroom in case there is a fire.

   _____

7. Why should you stay low if there is smoke in the house?

   _____

8. Write down two things you can do at home to make it more fire safe.

   _____

It's a Whale Tale

Teacher Notes

Additional Content Area(s)

- language arts

Objective:

Students will

- identify the structure and function of different whale parts.

Materials Required:

- computer with Internet access
- pencil or pen

Web Site(s):

http://www.whaletimes.org/whapuz.htm

Time Required:

- 20–25 minutes

Teaching the Lesson:

- Attach this activity to a unit on mammals or cetaceans if possible. Link it to a classic story such as *Moby Dick*. In addition, you can discuss the plight of whales in modern times and the attempt by many to save them from extinction.

- As an enrichment activity, have students conduct an Internet search to find out information about a particular whale type. They can do presentations in teams so the whole class will learn about many whale species.

Name: _____ Date: _____

It's a Whale Tale

Do you know the different parts of a whale? Do you know what they are used for? Let's find out!

Go to:

http://www.whaletimes.org/whapuz.htm

Complete the whale quiz on this Web page. After you finish, write a sentence below that contains each correct answer.

1. _____

2. _____

3. _____

4. _____

5. _____

Bonus Question: What human organ is like the blow hole of a whale? Explain why.

_____

_____

Leonardo's Art and Science

Teacher Notes

Additional Content Area(s)

- social studies
- science

Objectives:

Students will

- examine paintings of Leonardo da Vinci.
- duplicate his writing style.

Materials Required:

- computer with Internet access
- pencil or pen
- painting/drawing supplies (optional)

Web Site(s):

---

http://www.mos.org/sln/Leonardo

http://www.mos.org/sln/Leonardo/LeonardoRighttoLeft.html

Time Required:

- 25–45 minutes

Teaching the Lesson:

- This lesson should come after an introduction to who Leonardo da Vinci was. A virtual museum visit to see his paintings via the Internet is a good idea as well.
- Help students discuss why and how Leonardo wrote his notes in such an unusual way.
- Explore modern scientific marvels that were first imagined by Leonardo.
- Students learning to draw and paint can use the strategies here to draw/paint in perspective as an optional activity.

Name: _____   Date: _____

Leonardo's Art and Science

Leonardo da Vinci was one of the most talented, imaginative people who ever lived. He was both an artist and a scientist. You can learn more about him at the Web sites below.

Go to:

http://www.mos.org/sln/Leonardo

Read the information on the Web page. Then answer the questions below.

1. During what time period did Leonardo live?

   _____

2. What was his most famous painting?

   _____

Go to:

http://www.mos.org/sln/Leonardo/LeonardoRighttoLeft.html

3. Why was Leonard's handwriting unusual and hard to read?

   _____

4. Why might Leonardo have written in this way?

   _____

Click on "try it yourself" and see what it's like to write like Leonardo!

5. Now write your name below the way you usually do. Then write it as Leonardo would!

   _____

   _____

Name That Tune

Teacher Notes

Additional Content Area(s):

- music

Objective:

Students will

- determine the titles of various well-known songs.

Materials Required:

- computer with Internet access
- pencil or pen

Web Site(s):

http://www.cyberkids.com/Games/musicquiz/musicdesc.html

Time Required:

- 25–35 minutes

Teaching the Lesson:

- The success of this lesson depends largely upon whether students have heard the songs before. You should check the selections yourself and see that they have been exposed to at least a handful of them before beginning.

- Be sure the students are aware that they are to write down the correct name of each song as they listen to each and get immediate feedback online.

Name: _____ Date: _____

Name That Tune

Do you have an ear for music? Are you good at remembering songs that you hear? Lets see if you can name and remember some popular songs.

Go to:

http://www.cyberkids.com/Games/musicquiz/musicdesc.html

Write down the correct names of each of the 15 songs that you will listen to.

1. _____

2. _____

3. _____

4. _____

5. _____

6. _____

7. _____

8. _____

9. _____

10. _____

11. _____

12. _____

13. _____

14. _____

15. _____

World of Art

Teacher Notes

Objective:

Students will

- match paintings to various artists.

Materials Required:

- computer with Internet access
- pencil or pen

Web Site(s):

---

http://www.thru.com/art/game/

Time Required:

- 25–35 minutes

Teaching the Lesson:

- Preview all the paintings on this Web page before doing this activity. There are two or three paintings that you may deem inappropriate for your students.
- This activity is for advanced students or pairs of students.
- Explain and show different paintings by classic/renaissance artists to students so they can see the similarities among styles before doing this activity.

Name: _____ Date: _____

World of Art

Artists who paint many different paintings often use the same style in their work. In this activity, you will look carefully at paintings done by several Italian artists. You will then see a different painting, and you have to try to match it to the artist.

Go to:

_____

http://www.thru.com/art/game/

_____

After you match the artists with the paintings, write them below.

Painting #1 _____   Name of Artist_____

Painting #2 _____   Name of Artist_____

Painting #3 _____   Name of Artist_____

Painting #4 _____   Name of Artist_____

Painting #5 _____   Name of Artist_____

Painting #6 _____   Name of Artist_____

Painting #7 _____   Name of Artist_____

Painting #8 _____   Name of Artist_____

Painting #9 _____   Name of Artist_____

Painting #10 _____   Name of Artist_____

Sketch It on the Web

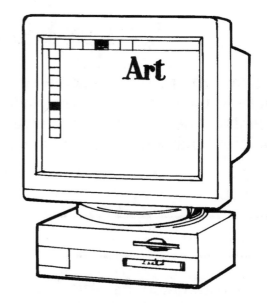

Teacher Notes

Objectives:

Students will

- sketch a drawing on the Internet.
- write stories about their drawings.

Materials Required:

- computer with Internet access
- pencil or pen

Web Site(s):

http://www.digitalstuff.com/web-a-sketch/

Time Required:

- 25–40 minutes

Teaching the Lesson:

- Be sure all students are comfortable using the drawing program online before they begin sketching their final pictures.
- Students will need to be creative but use simple figures due to the limitations of the program.
- They can submit their sketches online and receive some recognition if it is chosen in the ongoing contest at this Web site.

Name: _____ Date: _____

Sketch It on the Web

Here is your chance to show your talents on the World Wide Web! Start a new Web-a-sketch and create a picture. Take your time; it will take some practice to get good at it. When you are finished, write a story below about what is happening in your picture.

Go to:

http://www.digitalstuff.com/web-a-sketch/

Title of My Picture:

_____

Story of My Picture:

_____

_____

_____

_____

_____

_____

_____

_____

_____

_____

_____

Web Site Updates

Teacher Created Materials is dedicated to providing you with up-to-date links. To that end, you can use the link below for updates or changes to the URLs listed in this book.

http://www.teachercreated.com/updates/indmex.html

At the above page you will find updated links and a link to notify us of any dead ends you run into on the information superhighway. Please note that only links which have changed will be maintained at this site.

Changed URLs

_____

_____

_____

_____

_____

_____

_____

_____

_____

_____

_____

_____

_____

_____

_____

_____

_____

_____